Gender Trauma and The Healing of Tommy-Girl

Gabriel Orion Marie
(Veronica C. Wanchena)

Copyright © 2016 Gabriel Orion Marie

All Rights Reserved. No part of this publication may be reproduced, stored, transmitted, or disseminated in any form or by any means without prior written permission from Gabriel Orion Marie, aka Veronica C. Wanchena.

ISBN: 978-1629670669
Library of Congress Control Number: 2016936615

For Jean Cozier*, whose friendship is a golden thread in the fabric of my healing, and a bright joy in my life. Without her mentoring and support I may never have taken my first steps into the world as an artist and author.

*Founder and President of The Awakenings Foundation, Chicago, Illinois.

The Awakenings Foundation is dedicated to making visible the artistic expression of survivors of sexual violence. To learn more about this Foundation, visit their website at:

www.awakeningsfoundation.net

Acknowledgment

I would like to thank Sophia Prater, MS, for her questions that are included in this book. My responses to her are also part of her own research project.

Contents

Introduction
1

Gender Trauma
3

Boy Knocked Over
12

Seized
16

Tommy-Boy
18

I Can't
22

Exposure
26

Mirror
30

Oh My Brother
34

I am Going Now
36

Separate Pain Together
38

Medicine
42

Emerging
46

Tommy-Boy and Jesus
50

Her
54

All of Me/Self-Portrait of a Soul
56

About the Author
63

Other Books by the Author
65

Introduction

It was in the spring of 2015 at the Chopra Institute in Carlsbad, California, that I first met Veronica.

It was a week of personal discovery, and at first, we all kept to ourselves. Isolated, walls up, and not yet knowing the relationships that would be formed at this very special place.

As the first few days progressed, all of us were unraveling our own personal cocoons that kept us protected from the outside world. Each of our cocoons was uniquely woven based on our experiences and were created to hide our personal struggles. Veronica was the exception. Her open, loving, and optimistic outlook was engaging to everyone at the retreat.

As I began to learn more about her story, I was in total awe of what she had been through.

How could someone who had lived through so much darkness exude such a light—a light of hope, love, and peace?

Through many deep conversations during that week, she revealed to me her struggle with her gender perception. Knowing I was a gay man, she shared with me her confusion and questions about sexuality.

The discussions we had opened my eyes to an entirely different perspective. She didn't fit into any of the traditional categories of the LGTBQ community that so many of us struggle to find identity, acceptance, and community in.

Sexual, physical, and emotional abuse had wounded her gender perception so profoundly that it totally altered her ability to reconcile her soul with her biological, sexual, and spiritual self.

She had been forced to change who she was at the whim of her father, from boy to girl and back again, over and over. She protectively learned to manifest the essence of each gender with such fluidity in order to escape the torture she would endure if she didn't please her father's ever-changing desires.

Years of this constantly abusive cycle had not only caused confusion over her sexuality but also left her alone in a world where she wasn't sure how to act, love, or engage with those around her.

Anyone else I know would have ended up a tortured soul with an endless cocktail of antidepressant medication and no hope. But not Veronica...

Gender Trauma & The Healing of Tommy-Girl is the powerful story of Veronica's journey from the darkness into a world of hope, love, and peace. Through her painful retelling of her horrific experience and her profound artwork that lead to her recovery, she allows each of us to see past the darkness to witness the transformation of her soul. She reveals to us her path of recovery from the severe Gender Trauma she wrestled so deeply with. Along the way, we are allowed to bear witness to the healing powers of inner expression that are present when someone finally sheds the cocoon of self-protection and transforms into a beautiful creature of love and forgiveness.

Dustin Sparks
New York, NY

Gender Trauma

Gender Trauma is a phrase that came to me as I have thought about how to communicate my personal experience of deep pain and confusion that resulted from being sexually and emotionally tortured and brainwashed regarding my own body and gender. This book is about my healing from that specific trauma and the many attending issues around my sense of self that resulted from those traumas.

I want to mention that in *Going Sane*, the second book of my trilogy, I wrote a chapter called "The Penis Question." That chapter dives deep into the details of brainwashing and torture sessions in my early childhood, in which my father literally drove me insane by forcing me to become alternately a boy or a girl for him. (Throughout the whole trilogy, I share in words and images the actual details of abuse, torture, brainwashing, and other forms of emotional and psychological violence that crushed my mind, broke my heart, and decimated my sense of self.)

Since I published my trilogy several years ago, I have come even further along the road of healing, and I have moved into a deeper, more reflective perspective on the whole gender issue within me. The lens I am looking through now is not so much of an explicit, biographical, recounting of the abuse that I experienced. Rather, it is a progressive, retrospective understanding of how devastating, disabling, and painful Gender Trauma was for me, and how the gaping wounds that came from it affected every area of my life. Now, I also have an internal overview of how these wounds gradually healed through the inner work that I have done.

The hundreds of paintings that I did during my years of therapy now serve as an alphabet that I use to communicate different layers and nuances of my experience of sexual abuse, violence, trauma, and recovery. My paintings contain multiple meanings for me. Over the years, I have come to see how each painting can reveal vast amounts of information for my own enlightenment about my wounding and healing processes. I understand my paintings more deeply as the years go by; they reveal new insights at different stages of the journey. My relationship with them deepens, and what I observe and glean from them changes as I, the observer, continue to change.

Within these pages, I offer you my own personal experience and my reflection upon that experience. In all of my books and presentations, I aim to communicate solely from a place of self-referral. I know that there are as many experiences and perceptions of experiences as there are human beings. Although, at times, I feel a profound resonance with what someone else shares, I know that no person can ever entirely speak for another, regardless of the parallels. Each person's uniqueness—the singular, exclusive, expression of self—belongs to him or her alone.

The conundrum that I happily stumbled upon was this: The solitary uniqueness, this feeling of being all alone and utterly separate, is perhaps my greatest connection to every other human person. How amazing it has been to discover a magnificent communion with every human being, and every aspect of creation surfacing in the very place where I previously suffered a feeling of dreadful, solitary confinement! Processing my Gender Trauma has been such an odyssey for me...taking me from the dungeons of inner despair to a sense of understanding and connection with so many other people.

As I have journeyed through the shattering of illusions, followed by a re-awakening of previously numbed thought processing, a light has shone brightly on all of these areas of my self that I once feared. Love—in the form of wisdom, compassion, respect, and consciousness—has reached those places where I once groaned and grieved in my terror-stricken mind.

This love, this enlightenment, has startled me at times with its keen sharpness. Healing, as benevolent as it is, can unexpectedly slip between the bone and the marrow of my thoughts and beliefs, causing massive, sudden shifts that topple my old mental edifices in a flash and without warning. They have been and continue to be those life-changing "Aha!" moments that rock my world and catapult me into much saner and more peaceful places.

This same love has also comforted me at times with such a soft gaze of acceptance, understanding, and non-judgment that I have gradually allowed it to unbind me from the crippling, shaming chains of self-hatred. I have slowly learned how to *receive* love, with its myriad of faces and reflections. Self-possession and self-referral could emerge only after the toxic pain had been revealed, lanced, and grieved.

Looking through this luminous, reflective lens, I now recognize with awe the brilliance of my survival strategies that were misdiagnosed as insanity, time and time again. Now, I get glimpses of the phenomenal beauty and mastery that was called forth from my whole being as I desperately survived the impossible.

The title for this book, Gender Trauma & The Healing of *Tommy-Girl*, came to me in the early stages of writing it. I had originally thought about naming it *Tommy-Boy* because that was the name of one of my primary male Personas. But using the name *Tommy-**Girl*** more accurately communicates the gender trauma I suffered through.

In this book, I hope to convey, at least in part, how this agonizing gender abuse and Gender Trauma has morphed from psychotic, soul-splitting defeat into a powerfully harmonic assembly of qualities that I now know to be *Me*.

Throughout this book, I have included responses to questions that were asked of me by a university student who has used my story as a subject for a research paper about trauma recovery. Her questions were well-formed, and they triggered my mind and heart to further share my process of healing. The first two questions that she asked are a good launching pad for this book:

How has art played a role in your life, as it pertains to your experience of abuse?

Creating art emerged from within me, as a form of communication with my therapist, Dr. A. Early in therapy, when I was so frozen stiff with emotional trauma, I could not speak of the horrors that I was carrying inside of me. Even when I *did* try to speak of these horrors, my words felt empty, hollow, and completely inadequate. No matter how much I said with words, the torment, the terror, the memories, and the trauma stayed stuck inside of me.

My frustration was growing, along with dread and despair. I felt that I would never be able to really communicate to another human being what had happened to me and how my trauma had driven me to insanity and the brink of suicide.

Then one day, Dr. A., being keenly aware of my deep frustration, asked me if perhaps I might be able to draw or paint what I was trying to tell him. After my session, I went back to my room where I lived, found some old pencils and crayons and paper and—out of sheer desperation—I did my first drawing. It was a disturbing drawing. It was of a stomach full of penises.

My father had raped me for years and forced me to perform oral sex on him; he also sold me as a child prostitute to do this for strangers. For as long as I can remember, I had a sickening, nauseating, nasty, and ugly feeling in my stomach. It was the memory of all of those oral rapes. As a child, I really believed that they were all still in my stomach.

When that first drawing came out, it was the most cathartic and thrilling moment! When I saw the picture that I had drawn, albeit graphic and not easy to look at, my stomach felt a huge relief. For the first time in over 40 years, I was no longer nauseated. I was able to show the drawing to Dr. A., and I felt so proud that I was finally able to communicate a trauma in a way that felt real, true, complete, and accurate. I knew in my own body, in my own soul, that a picture speaks more than a thousand words. Drawing truly helped me to externalize the pain, where I could deal with it with the help of Dr. A. and not be trapped with it stuck in my body and mind.

Do you think there is a difference between a sexual abuse survivor and a sexual abuse victor?

Yes, Yes, Yes! My whole message is that I did not want to be only a survivor. I wanted to have a joyful, abundant, thriving life! And this is what is happening now, after more than 10 years of inner work. My experience of victory over trauma, abuse, darkness, terror, and insanity is real and thrilling to my core. Your question is very apropos. I have literally just written the following piece about that topic, and it is going to be part of my next book [this book] about Gender Trauma. I entitled this section "Victor." Here is my answer to your question:

Victor

My father was born weak, innocent, dependent, and vulnerable, just like every other human person who has ever come into the world. He was born to a dirt-poor immigrant family. They lived in a tar-paper shack in a small coal mining town in Montana. He was my grandparent's baby boy, the third of four boys. They named him Victor. He was baptized Victor.

Sixty-two years later, he died in a hospital in Minnesota. He had shriveled and shrunk with heart disease, kidney disease, and cirrhosis of all of his major organs. This was after having numerous heart attacks and six years of complicated medical issues, mostly stemming from decades of severe alcoholism and heavy smoking.

The life that man lived between his entry into and his departure from this world is one that profoundly wounded, terrorized, scarred, and damaged many people, including me. The violence and abuse that he inflicted upon me left me broken, mentally staggering, and painfully crazed.

His drunken rages terrified me daily, hourly, even after he had passed out or left town. Fear and dread of him was never absent, even when he was. His lordship over my physical and emotional existence was fierce, cruel, and completely devastating.

He was my father. He was lord and master of my existence until he died when I was 16 years old. He beat me, raped me, and mocked me. He sold me as a child prostitute to strangers in spooky hotel rooms. He and his evil cameraman friend created child pornography with me and other children who had been brought to the hotel by other men.

He hated me. He was ashamed of me for existing, it seemed. He told me that if he had a dog with face like mine, he would shave its ass and make it walk backwards. I believed him. You would not believe how many dogs I looked at throughout my childhood, trying to figure out what I looked like. That was the mirror that he held up to me. Since he had driven me insane, I honestly thought that is what I looked like. And it devastated me beyond belief.

He threatened me with death so often and so viciously that I began to wish that he would just make good with his threat and get it over with. The torture of wondering each day if I would be killed was almost worse than being alive. Almost. Except that being killed by him would mean that he had won.

One of the most debilitating forms of abuse that he inflicted on me was his sadistic demand that I become a boy or girl for him, on the spot, repeatedly, for years. It confused me to my core. He manipulated my mind and my body so systematically that I could switch like a magician in a split second to become whatever he was craving and hating at the moment.

My genius, my brilliance in surviving him was at its most breathtaking (and heartbreaking) in those moments. Yet it was in the endless hours, years, and decades later when I stood alone and paralyzed in front of my closet door, not knowing how to dress, that I felt that the poisonous effect would never end. It was when I needed to use the bathroom or when I looked in the mirror that the damaged surfaced. The knots of confusion were so numerous, so tight, and so twisted that unraveling them was impossible. The solution would come, but I discovered that it would never come at the level of the problem. I would eventually need to find a path of understanding that did not start with any gender definitions.

That I survived a tumultuous, premature, and dangerous birth circumstance was the first miracle of my life. That I survived the next 16 years of being his daughter and victim was a hundred thousand miracles. That I have had the courage and fortitude to spend four decades recovering my life from the heap of ashes it was when he died is several million more miracles.

As I mentioned earlier, my father's name was Victor. I always felt sick at the sight or the mention of his name. If anyone asked me what my father's name was, nausea would overtake me as the name "Victor" would reluctantly come out of my mouth. I hated his name.

As soon as I learned to read, I became fascinated by and obsessed with dictionaries, words, meanings, languages, and etymologies. I perceived words viscerally, and I would wrestle with ones that triggered revulsion in me. It is difficult to describe that strange, muscular, cellular power struggle, but I see it now as having been an ingenious way of transferring some of my battles into arenas where I had a chance of winning.

Here is what the Merriam-Webster's Dictionary says about my father's name:

Full Definition of VICTOR

: one that defeats an enemy or opponent

— **victorious** *adjective*

Origin of VICTOR

Middle English, from Anglo-French, from Latin, from *vincere* to conquer, win; akin to Old English *wīgan* to fight, Lithuanian *veikti* to be active

First known use: 14th century

Synonyms

beater, conqueror, master, subduer, trimmer, vanquisher, whipper, winner

Antonyms

loser

What a definition! It very accurately describes my perception and experience of my father while he was here on earth.

Yet here I am now, a woman of peace, strength, blessings, and great joy. Definitions, etymologies, synonyms, and antonyms are swirling around in the spaces of my mind and heart as I write about a man whose force ended up working *against* him and *for* me. I smile now at a name that once caused me to cringe with trepidation and dread but has now become a title I have earned in overcoming a mountain of evil.

Part of my journey has been the publishing of books and giving public presentations about my experience of wounding and healing from severe abuse and trauma. These have been huge personal achievements that have furthered my liberation from the past. But by far, my greatest achievement, the most amazing feat in my life thus far, is that I have come to a place where I deeply love and enjoy life! I did not settle for survival; I insisted on thorough healing.

I know that deep suffering has carved into me a greater capacity for joy than I would have had if I had never been so hurt, simply because contrast has created that capacity. Extreme contrast has also given me an intense vividness of sensations as my consciousness has awakened through this recovery process. I love more. I am grateful for more. I enjoy more. I see more. I understand so much more.

It would be an enormous omission if I did not include in this book the fact that I have completely forgiven my father. I have forgiven him in order to free myself from the poison of hatred and resentment. I have forgiven him because it does not nourish my soul or give me joy to harbor even justified rage and hatred.

Forgiveness has distinctly become majestic, powerful wings on my spirit. They have grown from the tiniest feathers, one by one, as I thoroughly and honestly traversed the necessary years of embracing and expressing every drop of rage, hatred, and crushing disappointment. Finally, I became tired of hatred and it no longer served me. Refreshment came with letting go, leaping of the cliff of my rights, and soaring over new lands with wider vistas, broader horizons, and stunning views.

Who is Victor now?

Boy Knocked Over

Boy Knocked Over

Here is one look into the window of my soul when I was a child. This painting is one of the most tender boy Personas that I created. I did not know how to create an authentically tough boy, so instead I created a heart big enough to withstand and grieve the repetitive murder of the children that it continuously gave birth to.

This is a painting of me when I was a young girl, trying to be a boy. This was how it felt to be knocked over inside by the cruelty of the demands that were put on me and the insanity that those demands drove me into. Through these years of healing, that place of insanity has become a place of deep seeing, where this boy—this girl who was forced to pretend she was a boy—is alive and well.

This part of me now has a great capacity for, and quality of, resilience. I bounce back very quickly from setbacks, triggers, and trip-ups. This transformation has come through my complete, conscious acceptance of all that I felt from the moment of impact that this painting depicts, through the psychotic space that I was toppling through in my mind and the thudding blow of landing on the floor of my soul.

One of my childhood friends had a toy called a Bop Bag. It was a balloon-like clown that would receive a punch, hit the floor, and pop back up again. I remember being fascinated by this toy and playing with it for long spells. It was hypnotic to me. I internalized that capacity to be knocked over and to rise up again, seemingly unharmed.

Of course, I was only *seemingly* unharmed. Every psychic blow hurt me immensely, and it caused severe damage. But at least for the time that I was in the environment of abuse, I could appear to pop back up. Looking back, I appreciate and understand my fascination with that toy. It was such a striking symbol of what I was enduring, and it mirrored for me what I needed to do in response to the repeated violence.

Even as I write this, I feel waves of the staggering grief and the most exquisite, tender love that I felt as a child, punching that clown in the face. Begging it to teach me. Begging it to help me survive my father.

Seized

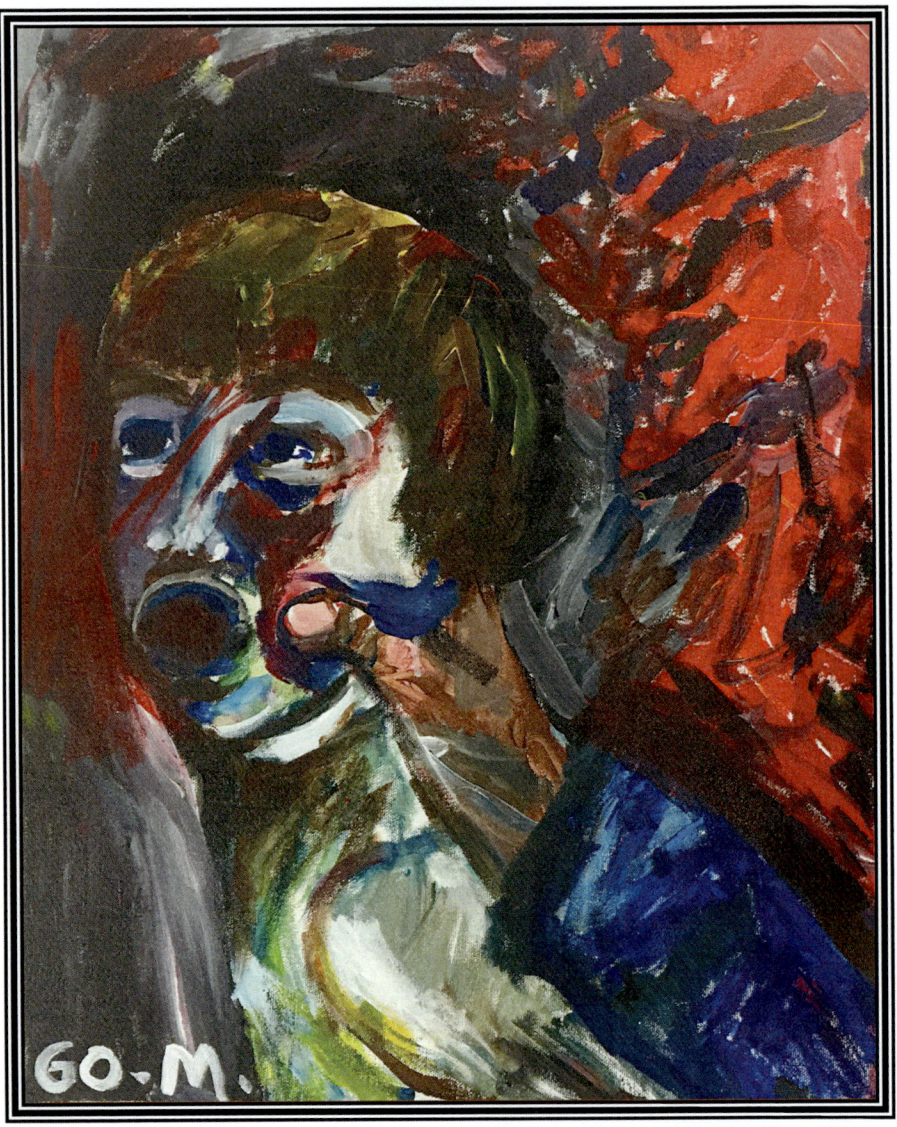

Seized

Throughout my years of therapy, I needed to be willing to look into the mirror of this intense terror that I carried inside of me. I saw how the threads from the fabric of my childhood terrors had become a gravely knotted and frayed nervous system that riddled my adulthood with this seized and frozen response to life. My father would seize me, suddenly and without warning. When one lives in perpetual fear, the concept of warning does not exist.

Holding my breath was an instinctual, biological response to being seized. Not knowing who I was—male or female—seized me further, tightening all of the muscle groups in my body. Being held by my neck, pressed against a wall, and ordered to be a boy drove my true self into hiding. It forced the emergence of survival instincts to animate my body like an unfeeling puppet through the deadly obstacle course of my childhood.

Gender Trauma and the wounds that it imprinted in my whole being have required enormous grieving. Grieving the years of confusion, distress, insanity, and loss. Being seized with anxiety for so long tightened my chest so fiercely that it felt like a cement wall. I have had to work very diligently to practice taking more and more air into my lungs. I could not cry and hold my breath at the same time. Recovery came as I allowed air into my lungs, one partial breath at a time. Deep breaths involuntarily became heavy sobs of grief, relief, and catharsis.

Years of acceptance, letting go, and trust have transformed this part of me. This child...this boy, this terrified girl...has become a warmhearted, deeply breathing, contemplative aspect of my soul.

Tommy-Boy

Tommy-Boy

Entering into the core and the center of this Gender Trauma, this private bleeding wound, I repeatedly encountered Tommy-Boy, huddled in the corner of my psychic structure. Tommy-Boy appeared on this canvas in this position, his arms and chest forming the shape of a heart, as if to whisper and point out to me that this trauma resided in my heart.

The methods that my father used to manipulate my genitals and torture my mind with repetitive questions and demands regarding my anatomy and gender severed almost all of the instinctive and innate connections and identifications with my body.

My privates always hurt, and they often bled as if weeping blood. Being wounded so enormously in my physical privates also stripped me of any concept of interior privacy. A raped body is a raped soul. An invaded mind exiles itself from itself. No privacy in my body and no privacy for my inner self meant that there were no boundaries within which I could create a stable identity. My personality framework was much like a wobbly skeleton of a building: Exposed. No walls. No touches of comfort. Not a place that I could ever think of as "home." Life was like a terrible play, and I had to constantly change the props and costumes that I was wearing. It all felt so unreal, so unfair, so untrue, and so critically unstable.

I was never safe from my father's grip or from the seizing, paralyzing consequences of his hatred of me during those years.

I discovered that in the healing process, I required concentrated times of privacy to form an identity and an understanding of self. The natural processes of maturation—whereby an increase of privacy is normally sought and boundaries foster the blossoming of personhood and authentic self-expression—had been demolished in me by sustained invasion and exploitation. With no ballast in my identity, I was completely ungrounded.

In order to recover my life, I needed to embrace this entire predicament, and I needed to do most of the inner work alone, in private. I discovered along the way that it was imperative that I create consistent, structured times of dependable privacy. These gaping, painful gender wounds required a gentle, safe, and quiet solitude to heal.

Alone time gave me the space that I needed to practice breathing and to be very present for my many Personas that surfaced with their pain, anger, confusion, and trauma. Cultivating alone time was no easy task. It demanded consciousness, courage, and commitment from me to be alone with this pain that had driven me insane. I did not shrink from this task, and its rewards appeared almost immediately.

The great poet Rumi wrote these beautiful, consoling words: "The wound is the place where the Light enters you." After entering and staying with the consequences of this Gender Trauma for many years, I woke up one day with the comforting realization that Tommy-Boy was the quality of my heart that stayed vulnerable and tender, rather than the embodiment of the cruelty that my heart suffered.

Can you explain your process of creating an image?

It always began with either a physical sensation (as in the nausea I described earlier), or an intense emotion, or a picture in my mind.

In the beginning, these were always unpleasant, painful, often tormenting sensations, memories, or feelings that I was plagued with. Depending on the Persona who was creating the image, the process might be a little different. Lume was one who tried to be really exacting, so her process was more deliberate and tense.

Gabriel Orion Marie, on the other hand, created very differently. He would leap up off a chair, grab the palette and paints, and wildly and very quickly practically hurl a painting onto the canvas in a matter of minutes.

Tommy-Boy would emerge and paint quietly at night when none of the rest of me was looking. I would wake up see a painting on the canvas signed by Tommy-Boy and gasp! He was really shy and didn't even want the rest of me to be present when he painted.

Although each part of me chose a different process, the healing effect was universal. Each part of me felt enormous relief, catharsis, and even joy about getting the darkness OUT.

I Can't

I Can't

This is the painting that I chose for the cover of my book, *Going Sane*. I chose it because *going sane* was precisely what I felt I could not do. Finding peace, sanity, and authenticity regarding my gender felt impossible. Torture, in all of the forms that I experienced it, entailed double binds. The double binds stayed with me between torture sessions, repeating themselves over and over, tormenting my mind. They continuously haunted me, chased me, and defeated me. In this way, my abusers perpetuated their control over me by planting these double binds in my mind, knowing I would continue to torture myself with the insolubility of them.

If I identified myself as a woman, I experienced wild, raging, hysterical upheaval inside of me. I had created way too many serious male Personas to get away with that.

If I identified myself as a man, the immediate and urgent conflict was the gaping absence of male anatomy in my given body, which was humiliating and crushing to me.

If I identified as any substantially defined combination (of inner and outer male and female manifestations) I felt dreadfully trapped and pigeonholed. I felt hounded by the monster in this painting that hovered over my gender-traumatized self, threatening total disintegration via the unrelenting stress of these eternally unsolvable riddles.

The physical gender abuses and tortures that I survived had dismembered the psychosocial anatomy of gender in me as well, creating a massive abyss between me and every person I so desperately wanted to be in relationship with. Those inhumanities put me in a psychosocial solitary confinement from which it took me years to emerge. Outwardly, I was always very social, gregarious, and loving. I sincerely attempted to bond with countless people. Inwardly, however, my solitary agony kept the most authentic elements of my soul and personality from truly bonding with anyone else's.

Recovery of my true self required me to enter the place in my soul where this painting was a living reality. I had to muster the courage to stand up and take from my face the bloody mask of humiliation and shame. I had to lift up my head and be willing to make long, open, sustained eye contact with the monster.

One day, not unlike the important realization that Dorothy and Toto had when they saw a frightened, quivering man pretending to be the Great Oz, I stumbled upon the truth that this monster was actually a long-dead memory of my long-dead father, making threats from long ago that were now empty.

That is how "*I can't*" became "I can and *I will.*"

Exposure

Exposure

In dealing with these most delicate, painful, and complicated gender-abuse and Gender Trauma issues, I felt alarmingly—and terrifyingly—*exposed*. It was not until I was firmly established in a trusting relationship with Dr. A. that I dared to begin bringing these experiences and conflicts into the therapeutic arena. I needed to see them and explore their meaning with a safe person. One by one, I released them from my psyche, the nearly exploding pressure cooker where they had been stored. One by one, I laid them out in the open and rigorously honest arena of my therapy sessions.

Exposure triggered shame spirals, panic attacks, and urges for self-harm, yet it was absolutely crucial for my recovery that I leave nothing consciously hidden. My secrets were killing me. They had driven me insane. Crucial, post-session aftercare was necessary when I had delved deep into these wounds and exposed them. I had to perform soothing, gentle rituals that would help me regain a sense of safety after existing in such vulnerability. I used prayers, candles, bath salts, swimming, heat and light, soothing hot teas, soft foods, and deep sleep, which all helped.

I looked deep into the eyes of the young boy Persona here in this painting. I felt all of this pain, all of the darkness that was a bloody, sticky tar covering my mind.

The following definition, along with its synonyms, accurately communicates what the alchemic processing of these deep torments entailed:

Exposure:

noun

1. the act of exposing, laying open, or uncovering
2. disclosure, as of something private or secret
3. an act or instance of revealing or unmasking
4. presentation to view, especially in an open or public manner

Synonyms of Exposure

Disclosure, vulnerability, betrayal, defenselessness, nakedness, peril, revelation, unmasking, unveiling

Thoroughly exposing these most intimate struggles, traumas, and torments resulted in freedom. The critical resource was courage. Uncompromising, unyielding courage lived out, one moment at a time, for the years that I needed to toil to attain the stunning prize of freedom.

This wounded place of exposure has now become the part of me that lives in vast open spaces, comforted by soothing, warm, gentle light. Furthermore, this formerly unbearable pain of exposure has been transformed into self-confidence and self-possession.

In regard to your art making, has there been something that has really helped you move forward?

Yes. I have learned over the years to simply breathe and allow the internal (and often unconscious) communication become externalized and conscious. Creating art, writing books, and giving talks are all very much the same process for me. They each require a commitment to presence, to breathing, to allowing what is invisible to become manifest in the visible world through a form of creativity.

Initially, my creation of art was like uncontrolled, projectile vomiting of the pain and experiences. It was necessary for it to be like that back then because what was surfacing was so toxic. I often referred to my process of painting as mental and emotional vomiting. That may sound like a really gross analogy, but stop and think of a time when you were really nauseous, perhaps from food poisoning. Your whole body becomes queasy, clammy, and you feel ill all over. You can't think straight because you are so sick to your stomach. It is all rumbling around inside of you and then, all of a sudden, your body begins to heave it all out.

It might feel awful as it is coming out, but you immediately feel a whole lot better because the poison has been purged. Then you can begin to recover. As long as the poison is inside of you, it keeps you very, very sick.

Very important for my healing process was paying attention to the psychological and biological clues that something was trying to surface or emerge. I learned to recognize the toxic feelings, the psychic nausea, the emotional cramping that would build up until, suddenly, my soul would heave out a painting.

Non-judgment of what came out of me enabled me to have the courage to let out all of these things that I felt so deeply ashamed of, afraid of, and guilty for. (Part of what created the insanity was a deep, dark guilt for needing to communicate the ugly things that were done to me.)

Becoming the "observer of the creative process" was scary to me. Standing in front of my easel, literally watching my hand and the brush create a communication and just allowing it to be without trying to change what was appearing, was both terrifying and shocking at times. It was important that I watch as a bystander as the expression came out of me, instead of trying to force it out or drag it out. It was equally important that I did not try to stifle or stop a painting from coming out, no matter how disturbing it was, no matter how afraid I was of its content.

Keeping self-imposed restrictions was like trying to swallow vomit that was half way out. It was horrendous. I tried to stop things from coming out early on, but that caused a horrible psychological choking feeling that disabled me. By contrast, the amazing, cathartic relief I felt when I *did* let the gory details out was so liberating and healing. Sorry if this is a bit disgusting, but let me tell you, this is the most accurate way I can honestly answer your questions.

Mirror

Mirror

Mirrors always haunted me and terrified me. They upset me, tormented me, mocked me, and scared the daylights out of me. For decades, I spent extensive amounts of energy avoiding mirrors and reflections of my body.

Gender trauma and Dissociative Identity Disorder (DID) created a kaleidoscopic sense of self for me that was entirely unstable. I had a completely unpredictable expectation of what I would see in a mirror, and it never matched biological reality in terms of gender, age, size, appearance, etc. Because of this, every glimpse of my reflection startled and shocked me. Seeing a reflection of myself in a mirror or even in a window or a glass door was always a very jarring bombshell. I honestly never saw what I *expected* to see, and I often felt like I had just been shot through my brain.

During therapy, there were many times when I stood in front of a mirror in my room, trying to paint what I saw. It never failed that by the time I had finished the image, a different Persona had popped out, was bewildered by what it saw, and wondered who was on the canvas.

I lived for a very long time with this completely unresolved. Healing took place very gradually in this area, and self-knowledge and self-possession came in tiny increments. I started by finding one thing that every Persona agreed upon, like a love of coffee or swimming. Coffee was a good gathering place because it was part of my daily routine. I would sip my coffee in the dark, early hours of the morning before sunrise and let myself feel a unified physical experience.

Recovery of a unified reflection was supported by the consistent, respectful, accepting gaze of Dr. A., who never wavered in his quiet, steady welcoming of me regardless of which Persona I presented as. He showed no preference for one part of me over another. At one point, I realized that to him, I was only *one* person, *one* client. That realization puzzled me and intrigued me, and as it stayed with me,

Dr. A. became a mirror for me—one that I became more and more comfortable looking into. I began to wonder what it was like for him to have me in his office. Imagining myself in his chair became a first step into objectivity for me, where the reality of being one person, a whole person, could start to take shape as a real possibility.

Have you ever created an image you disliked? Why?

This is a hard question to answer. The core answer is no. Everything I ever drew or painted contributed to my healing. Every image, especially some of the most disturbing ones, had the effect of pulling the ugly, icky, distressing, paralyzing, isolating, traumatizing experiences out of me. You see, the memories were like torturers who lived inside of me, causing me to repeatedly relive the abuse for decades after my father died.

It was the act of externalizing the experiences on paper and canvas that gave me power over them, because I was exposing them. I was telling on my dad. I was telling on the others who had done horrendous things to me.

Sometimes, one Persona might not like a painting that another one created. For example, Lume would create a painting that exposed Gabriel's resistance or anger, because she knew that he was afraid to acknowledge it himself.

Painting explicit memories or events was sometimes a way for one Persona to reveal something to another Persona.

The other thing I would say is that although I never really disliked anything I created, I often feared the reality that it was communicating. I was also scared to death of anyone other than Dr. A. ever seeing my paintings. In fact, during my early years of therapy, I had planned to destroy each painting after I had used it to communicate to Dr. A. When I told him this, he very wisely offered to store them in a locked closet in his office, and he assured me that they would be private and safe. His pledge allowed me to postpone any decisions about keeping them or destroying them. Dr. A. felt strongly that one day I would want to have them, but he also respected my fear of anyone but him seeing them in the meantime.

His foresight about this was very providential indeed. He saved them for me for several years until I had a place of my own where I felt safe to keep them. I also had a good camera, and at one point, I decided to take pictures of each of my paintings so that I could have a digital copy of everything.

Some years later, when I moved from Canada back to my hometown in the USA. I had a rather intense breakdown. I had all my original paintings with me. I was suddenly paranoid and sick about having all of these dreadful images so close to the actual, geographical places where my abuse had happened. I was terrified of my siblings or family members ever seeing them. I didn't want anyone from the next generation of my family to know how horrible it had been. I was afraid that our family history would poison my nieces and nephews if they ever found out how horrible it had been.

I destroyed over 200 of my originals that day. I really cannot even write much about those hours. All I remember is being in a washing sweat, crying, and ripping up painting after painting into small pieces, then driving them to a recycle depot and dumping all of the torn paper and canvases into a big dumpster.

I have had to grieve my way through my actions of that day. I have had to forgive myself for what I did, and also understand that for some reason, it must have been something that I had to do.

Thankfully, as I said, I have digital copies of everything. I also have around 100 originals, minus the ones that have been purchased. Creating, saving, destroying, keeping, selling, and publishing my art has kept me on a very interesting journey. My relationship with my art has traversed many twists and turns along the way.

Oh My Brother

Oh My Brother

There came a point in my life when all of the male Personas in me collapsed and seem to die. The physical evidence of not being male was becoming overwhelmingly stacked against them. I was beginning to go sane and become more integrated in my physical body. Becoming an apparent and profoundly painful concept to me was the realization that these many Personas inside of me were brilliant creations that had kept me alive during severe trauma, but were now hindering me from a stable life.

The female Personas did not take this any easier than the male ones did. For the former, the loss of powerful, smart, courageous brothers/comrades was frightening.

Neither the male nor female aspects of me were able to understand how the merging and unifying of self would happen, or if it even would. When the inner boys collapsed, it felt like a dreadful death.

While grieving the loss of the boys, I very well may have despaired had I known that before long, the female Personas were going to collapse, too. Personas are Personas, regardless of their expression. My unified self could only come forth as I released my fierce attachments to what and who I thought myself to be up to that point.

I am Going Now

I Am Going Now

Here something new is starting to happen. A strong male Persona (or possibly many male Personas symbolized by one) appears to have died. In my mind, I saw a female figure rise out of his loins.

The words that Jesus said to his Apostles when He was ascending to Heaven kept repeating in my mind: "I am going now to prepare a place for you." Standing at my easel, I was having some sort of a spiritual experience. I included some clouds in this painting into which this female figure would ascend. She needed to travel high above her earthly experience to find the place where my whole being could exist in some kind of harmony and unity.

For all of the collapsing of selves that had been happening inside of me, I still clung to a thought that somehow, these collapses were not really death, but rather some sort of inner shifting of consciousness. I mean, these aspects of me were operational successes. The ingredients that I had used to create them were courage, resiliency, genius, and a host of phenomenally strategic survival skills. Maybe it was only the containers that were collapsing, and maybe the contents of the containers would remain and somehow be arranged in a new being.

Yet, my healing required that I accepted the *feeling* of many deaths. It required that I be willing to exist with the disorienting feelings that went along with losing all sense of who I was.

During some of those months and years, I felt like I was just a chaotic jumble of verbs, adjectives, and names. Deep in the darkness of those times, the one word that never ceased to float around inside me was **love**. I knew that if I could keep love alive, one day all would be well.

Separate Pain Together

Separate Pain Together

So, if it was not death, what was it? Sometimes, it felt like "separate pain together," and there was no other way to describe it. In this painting, there has been a lot of healing in both the male and female parts of me. But the male aspects and the female aspects of me are both crying blood. Blood is coming out of their eyes, revealing that their vision is still wounded, still unhealed. Neither gender in me can really see things clearly because both genders are so wounded.

The male parts of me suffered tremendous amounts of mental anguish. From years of being brainwashed and needing to come up with survival strategies in response to horrendous forms of Gender Trauma and torture, the male parts carried insanity.

The female parts of me carried much more physical pain, especially in the lower half of my body. Those female aspects of me lived with physical flashbacks of bodily torture. Their genitals nearly always hurt. Talking about what had happened and painting about it usually caused an upheaval of extremely painful physical sensations. This happened in increasing intensity as therapy went deeper and deeper into my wounds. These painful bodily sensations subsided only after years of inner work, which allowed for the emergence of a new consciousness and a new sense of being in my body.

Gender trauma and gender abuse were so extensive that they complicated all of the other layers of trauma that I endured. They robbed me of a place of being where I could face the world, face the trauma, face the work, face the healing. I literally had no place to call home. No place to call *me*.

True and trustworthy healing transpired, and with that, the merging of inner qualities and the disintegration of emotional and psychic walls that separated them. Those dividing walls once saved me from being fully conscious of an overwhelming amount of trauma. After childhood, however, those same walls fostered an illusory sense of autonomy in each of my Personas, and that no longer served me.

One of the things that I loved about this painting was that the male aspects and the female aspects were both beautiful. They loved each other. They wanted to be together. They completed one another. Over the years, I had experienced huge conflicts among some of my Personas, often resulting in their arguing, hating, accusing, and despising each other. This painting was a sign of hope for me that I was making progress in the healing of Gender Trauma and gender abuse. I was starting to come together inside.

I was slowly going to discover who I was, and somehow, it was going to include everyone.

Medicine

Medicine

Now I could see that these male and female aspects in me were maturing. All of the inner work—sessions with Dr. A., painting, praying, writing—was helping. Physical therapies were crucial at this stage, too. I swam several times a week. I took long baths with detoxifying salts and oils, every single day. I was eating healthy and starting to sleep better.

Self-care had never come naturally to me, nor was it particularly pleasant or easy in the beginning. Besides being a new discipline that I incorporated into my daily life because I believed that it would help, it was also frightening to me. It was stressful at the time to take the medicine of self-care, and I had mixed feelings about all of it. Doing these things for myself *seemed* to be very selfish, and according to what I had believed, that was morally wrong. I had to learn that taking good care of oneself was a good thing to do—that it was a way of honoring the gift of Life.

This painting reveals that my male and female selves have left the survival mode of adolescence and have become adults. There is still red blood between them and around them, signifying that they have not united completely. The medicine that they need to take is also red, signifying that it, too, is going to be painful.

Healing sometimes required taking painful, bitter medicine. Going sane often felt as disorienting as going insane had been. It was such a reversal, an about-face way of seeing everything. But I also want to say that it was important for me to regularly remind myself that the pain of healing was not equal to, or in any way a parallel, of the pain of being abused. The pain of healing was different. It was the pain of stretching past my contracted state of mind. The pain came mostly in the form of fear or deep grief, both of which I had to wholly process my way through.

Dr. A. did everything that he could to support and encourage me as I made self-care choices to ease the stresses, which the healing work so often required. I learned through the years to dance with the process and to balance the really difficult weeks with more rest and more self-care. That is a skill that I continue to use in life, and it serves me very well.

It gave me to joy to see in this painting that both parts of me were beautiful, strong, and healthy looking. The woman's breast is slightly detached, because she has not fully accepted her womanhood yet. She is getting close, though. The breast is in the right place, and it is beautiful. It would fall into place as soon as a few more steps had been taken and after a few more doses of medicine had been swallowed, digested, and metabolized.

The male part of me seems strong, fit, and very gentle. His back is turned, because he is not quite ready to admit and consent to not having male anatomy. (At the time of this painting, I was still not entirely ready to forfeit the illusion that I needed to be physically male to be strong, and to be who I was.)

Emerging

Emerging

Healing from Gender Trauma is emerging from the layers of inner work that I have done for so many years. This healing has required me to work through each of the many layers of the trauma.

- I have faced the years of feeling that I am a **Boy Knocked Over**, inside.

- I have worked through the depths of contraction and the terror of being **Seized**.

- I have found, and integrated the qualities of **Tommy-Boy** into the fabric of being Me.

- I have done the impossible. I have taken *I Can't* and made it into I Can and I *Will*.

- I have allowed **Exposure** to become part of my healing. By allowing the light and air to enter into the deepest caverns of my being, I have left nothing and no one behind.

- I have dared to look into the **Mirror** that life has held up to me. I have been willing to look into all of the fragments of mirrors that I have found, and I have retrieved those fragments and helped to meld them into the one image of being that I am.

- I have grieved all of the losses, deaths, and disappointments that I have encountered along the path of recovery. I have loved myself through each stage.

- I have transcended the suffering of Gender Trauma, and I have found a higher place of consciousness where *I Am Going Now* to become all of me.

- I have worked harmoniously with the male and female aspects of myself, witnessed my own **Separate Pain Together**, and come to the place of embracing of all of me.

- I have metabolized the **Medicine** of this therapeutic journey that I have been involved in, and in doing so, I have found healing, relief from suffering, and joy in being.

Now, the new me is **Emerging**. This me is fresh, innocent, and waking up into a conscious world where new joys and opportunities are awaiting me.

Tommy-Boy and Jesus

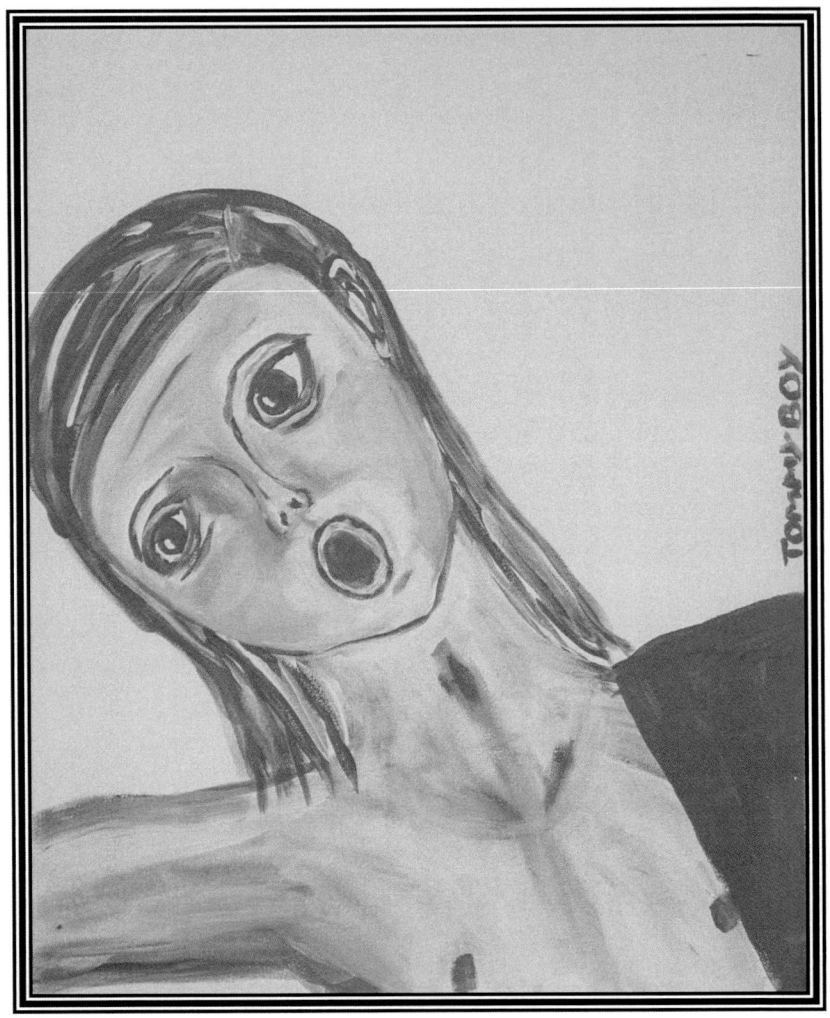

Tommy-Boy and Jesus

Healing could become a thorough experience only with the integration of my spirituality throughout the entire process. I have shared many times in my books and presentations some of the experiences that I had, from a very young age, of Angels and other invisible beings that visited me and helped me.

Jesus Christ has been central, though not exclusive, in my experience of spirituality and other non-material beings. All of my Personas always profoundly identified with Jesus Christ in His suffering and death. In this painting, I was portraying Tommy-Boy—a young male Persona in me—as he mirrored the Christ whom he regularly conversed with in prayer and in visitations. Tommy-Boy's arms were outstretched in cruciform fashion, and his mouth was open because he was singing of his communion, his connection with Jesus.

The passion, death, and resurrection of Christ have been a model of my own journey as I processed abuse, cruelty, violence, and every kind of torment that I endured. The path of Christ gave me a model of transcendence, healing, and victory over everything that crushed me.

My healing was not a "miracle." My recovery of a stable and peaceful sense of self did not come from anyone or anything outside of me; it emerged from deep within my core, invisible self, where I am connected to all that Is. Many times during the years of therapy, I begged for a miracle and argued with God and the Universe. One of the most pressing questions that I asked God was "Why don't You just heal me—instantly and completely—since I truly believe that you are able to?"

The response that reached my heart was "Because I want you to experience the dignity of participating in your own resurrection." As the years have passed, I am extremely grateful for this arduous path that has required so much of my own effort, commitment, and fortitude. Had I been healed magically, instantly, I would have then been a victim of a miracle, still lacking any connection to my own inner power of recovery.

I know that forces greater than me have been at work in my life from the moment of my conception. I know and love those forces of love, and I call them Abba, Father, Jesus, Spirit, Mother, Mary, Gabriel, Michael, and a myriad of others.

I am part of them, and they are all part of me. They reveal and reflect to me that my whole being--my gender and my lifetime of struggle with gender--is loved, honored, respected, and beautiful in all of its expressions.

Right now, here on earth, my bodily form is female and I love and respect this body of mine. My inner self is a beautiful, coherent mosaic of qualities that some call masculine or feminine, but I call them Me. And all of them are welcome and embraced.

Her

Her

This painting is a reflection of the amazing healing from the Gender Trauma. In this painting, I have peered into the mirror of my femaleness. I see what my femininity looks like to me. It is not a self-portrait of my physical body, but a self-portrait of the female Personas who have found peace and grounding in being connected to the physical body of a woman, and the nonphysical nuances of being biologically female.

I have taken back the rights over my body, and I have removed the judgments and condemnations of my body that I absorbed from my father. I have freed myself from measuring my body according to the messages from society and the media.

This peace has only come about through first going deep into the wounds, grieving them, expressing them, painting them, releasing them, and allowing my new self to emerge gradually and gently. I have allowed the dreadful wounds to heal in the alchemic fire of love, compassion, courage, and truth with God, my Witness, and myself.

All of Me/Self-Portrait of a Soul

All of Me/Self-Portrait of a Soul

This is the painting that I have chosen as my signature painting and my logo because I feel it most accurately communicates the wholeness of my self. It is beautiful and handsome; it could be male or female. It is all of me. It is the most real image of who I feel myself to be.

Tommy-Boy and Jesus are One. I am discovering that perhaps Tommy-Boy has been the Christ hidden within me all along.

I have found *Her*. She is restored to the kind of beauty that she was created with, and she is alive and well.

All of Me has come together. Now, all of the things I do—my books, my presentations, my art—are making incarnate the *Self-Portrait of a Soul*.

Compare your artwork in the beginning of your recovery and in the present and what has changed for you? And has anything stayed the same?

In the beginning, my artwork was solely my communication with my therapist. It was very private, and it was pretty much limited to painting and drawing. Now my creative work includes writing, speaking, and creating presentations.

In the beginning, my artwork was my autobiographical story that I told my therapist.

Now my artwork is part of the alphabet that I use to share a much more reflective perspective on the deepest effects and intricate healing processes in my experience of both abuse and recovery.

Instead of being a very private communication between a client and therapist, my artwork now is something that I openly and publicly share to offer hope, encouragement, and living proof that profound healing is really possible even from the most severe trauma.

I currently do not paint, but when I have the means for a studio and a place to live on my own, I will paint again. I look forward to what may spring forth now, because I do not have any deep angst or pain inside. I think that it will be the bursting forth of joy!

What has stayed the same is that it is all **communication.** Whether it is painting, writing, speaking ... it is all communication.

Where do you see yourself in 10 years?

With greater and greater joy, and deeper and deeper gratitude for my magnificent life. I see myself very much like I live now, only with a home to call my own, and a brightly sunlit studio and perhaps a brand new, shiny, red, sporty SUV that I can travel North America with.

I see myself traveling more of this amazing planet that God has made. I want to embrace the ground of every country that I possibly can. I want to meet and hug people from every country and experience their culture, their music, their food, their ideas, their language, their sorrow, and their joy.

I want to seek out everything that I think of as different, and find in everything all of the aspects that reflect perfect unity, complementariness, and completeness.

I want to be an alchemist of everything. I want to allow, accept, experience, and love every moment of my precious few years on this earth. I want to keep on finding the gift in every single moment.

That is the alchemy that I have been participating in all of these years, finding the gift in everything, even in the most dreadful, excruciating, cruel, and unthinkable tortures that I have endured. In all of those things, I have located the human capacity to survive and the indomitable spirit that will not cave in. I found my own courage in those tortures. I found my heart that refused to become a hater. I found my soul, and I discovered that it is a portion of the Eternal, whom I call God.

Who could ask for more?

What would you say to people who think that art therapy is not a valid form of psychology?

In my books, I lay out in very vivid and extensive ways how art became my voice. I believe that anyone in the helping professions would know about the human need for connection, communication, and understanding. Healing from trauma comes to a great extent through the communication of the trauma to a trusted person.

Here in the USA, in so many of our hospitals now, insurance companies are providing interpreters for people who not speak the language of the provider. The interpreter is the vehicle of communication between the patient and the doctor. Art was the interpreter—the communicator—between my doctor and me.

When words could not carry the intensity of my pain from my soul to my doctor, art became the strong, capable language that satisfied my need for articulation. Art is a language of the soul; in fact, in many ways, I believe that it may be a more valid channel for psychotherapy than the linguistic form that we are accustomed to because there is less probability of filtering the communication.

Perhaps people who think that art therapy is not a valid form of psychology have simply not had experience with that modality and are not familiar with it.

Poetry, music, art, drama, liturgy, and rituals, can all be extremely successful tools in the healing process. They are potentially charged with deep, and often subtle, expressions that make the difference between survival and thorough recovery.

Most importantly, I believe that anyone who has been victimized or traumatized should be offered whatever interpretive means are most beneficial to them. I do not believe in one modality over another.

I used music and drama, too. I conducted many funerals during sessions with Dr. A. to mourn the death of Personas and to express the inexpressible grief that was aching to be manifested. I employed cleansing rituals with bath salts and mud baths to help my body release toxic diseases that I carried. This was every bit as important for my healing as art and talking.

Milestones in the healing journey called for sacred liturgies that I would compose and officiate, either alone or with Dr. A.

Sometimes, a song had deep resonance in me, and I would listen to that song hundreds of times until it completed its work in my soul. I would bring my boom box to sessions with Dr. A., and he would listen to the same song with me over and over while it mysteriously healed another layer of my gaping wounds.

I would offer to sit with anyone who wants to know more, and let them ask me anything they wanted. I would present myself as living proof of not only the validity but also the amazing, alchemic possibilities that can grow out of art therapy and creative expressions when they are incorporated into the healing journey.

At what point did you start referring to yourself as an artist?

It never occurred to me that I was an artist until a few years ago. My drawings and paintings were the "communication board" of my traumatized body, mind, and soul that I used to speak with my therapist.

No one but Dr. A. ever saw my paintings until much later when I published my trilogy subtitled *Recovery From Incest Through Painting My Story*. I kept them hidden during the years of intensive therapy, because they were my private communications to my therapist. They were my secrets that I had shared with the one and only person whom I trusted at that time in my life.

I guess you could say that I thought of myself as a *communicator*, not an artist. It was several years later—when I began to show a few people whom I trusted that I had hundreds of paintings and drawings—that I began to discover that I was an artist.

In those early years, when I would show a painting or two to someone, the universal response was "I didn't know you were an artist!" (Neither did I!) So this is a very long answer to a simple question, but it is a significant question, and the answer has been evolving all through the years since I did that first drawing.

Another reason my answer is complex is that during those years, I had many Personas. I was diagnosed decades ago with DID (Dissociative Identity Disorder, back when it was called Multiple Personality Disorder, or MPD.) It was a child part of me, named Lume, who did those first drawings. Later, different Personas would pop out and do a painting or drawing. Each would sign their name, so my work has several different signatures, depending on who made a given painting or drawing. Lume, Tommy-Boy, Gabriel Orion Marie, Chris, Luminous Child——they all created images.

After deep integration, and after the publication of my first three books, I began to see that my expressions on canvas, and in words, did fall into the category of artistic after all. I have published five books, yet it still feels new to refer to myself as an author. I give presentations and do public speaking, yet I don't define myself as a speaker.

I now have *Author, Artist, and Speaker* on my business card, because those are several of the things that I am able to do and they are roles in which I share my heart with the world.

But they still do not define or contain me. If I had to use one term to define what I am, it would be "one who loves." I am one who seeks to spread kindness in the world.

I choose to love, with all my heart, as unconditionally and non-judgmentally as I am able.

What would you like to tell other survivors of sexual abuse who may still be struggling with their recovery?

I would remind them that it is evident that they have what it takes to recover, because they already survived the trauma. We prove that we have courage simply because we survived. It takes a lot of courage to survive severe abuse and trauma. After that, it takes another choice of exercising courage to recover.

I would say to anyone in the recovery process: Be kind and gentle with yourself as much as you can during the process. Self-care is maybe the most important and effective practice that creates the emotional fuel that you will need to keep you going for the long journey of healing.

In my experience, the one challenge in my life and my recovery that has required the most courage is that of accepting and enjoying JOY. You may think that I'm still a bit crazy to say that, but it is like this: When you are miserable, tormented, and living in constant PSTD and other manifestations of agony, you have nothing to lose.

Experiencing JOY was one of the most frightening things that I ever encountered, because suddenly and without warning, I had something precious to lose.

I have had to consciously work at increasing my joy threshold, step by step, because in the early stages of my healing, I could not tolerate very much joy. It felt dangerous. It felt like I was carrying a pot of gold through a dark alley. I felt so afraid of being robbed, or of somehow losing this new precious possession. I really had no idea what to do with joy. It was completely foreign to me.

In fact, when I got my first apartment at 48 years old, I was overwhelmed with emotion. I was shaking. I cried. I felt very vulnerable and my heart was pounding. I didn't know what was happening to me. Dr. A. said to me "That scary feeling that you have just might be joy!"

Indeed, it was joy. And I grew to embrace it and also not cling to it, letting it come and go as it does in every life. I have also learned to differentiate it from fear.

Joy and fear have a lot in common on the biological, experiential level. When I think of wild, huge roller coasters that I have ridden, and when I think of panic attacks, the feeling in my body is very similar; it is just that I emotionally classify or interpret one of them as fun and the other as scary.

Lastly, I would say to others who have survived terrible traumas and abuses: Don't settle for survival. Go for it all … Go for thorough healing and deep, abiding joy. Don't settle simply for symptom management, because there is so much that is available to the human spirit.

Go for the most wonderful life that you can imagine. And when you arrive there, you will see that an even more wonderful life is possible. Pursue that one.

Always remember to keep up with grieving. Even in healing, each step requires the grieving of the losses that we have just worked with. Grief is so different from misery. It is a cleansing acknowledgement of all that you have endured. Grieving is a sign of the respect that you show to your own soul, mind, and body, honoring all that they have carried of your burdens and wounds.

By keeping up with your grieving, you can keep your bucket free to receive the constant flow of this magical thing that we call life. Grieving is the ongoing release of what was, allowing you to open your whole being to what is and what can be.

About the Author

Gabriel Orion Marie (the pen name of Veronica C. Wanchena) is an author, artist, and speaker in the field of trauma recovery. Having survived years of severe abuse and the debilitating consequences, she now stands joyfully as a beacon of light witnessing to the power of the human soul to heal.

    Veronica used art as a primary tool of communication with her therapist Dr. A., and so recounts much of her story through the images that she created. The depth of thorough healing that she required called for enormous courage every step of the way. In her books, paintings, and presentations, she eloquently offers a vivid and profound inside view of her survival strategies and her healing process.

Other Books by the Author

Art as Alchemy: An Inside View of the Transformational Process

In *Art as Alchemy,* Gabriel Orion Marie (Veronica C. Wanchena), has written a brilliant synthesis that beautifully and profoundly takes the reader on a condensed version of her healing journey with her therapist, Dr. A.

In this potent little book, she articulates with great insight how her wounding damaged her, and she details the specific aspects of the therapeutic relationship that were most necessary for her full recovery. Her artwork in this book speaks as eloquently, simply, and openly as her words.

Dear Mom:
Forgiveness Unleashed

Courage, courage, and even more courage! That is the overarching quality of character that this journey required to free Veronica from the debilitating effects of abuse.

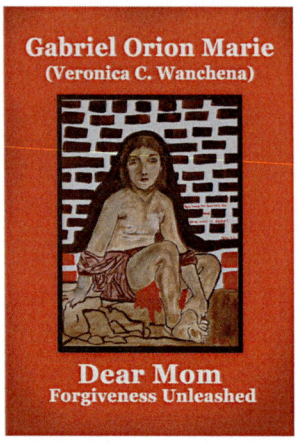

In *Dear Mom*, Gabriel Orion Marie (Veronica C. Wanchena) invites the reader to witness the inner challenges, struggles, and discoveries in this tremendous process of incarnating forgiveness of her mother. Heaping kindness onto someone by whom Veronica was deeply hurt brought profound liberation and an unimaginable new bond of love.

Recovery From Incest Through Painting My Story: A Trilogy

There are many themes in the areas of being wounded and finding healing from sexual abuse, incest, and torture, and for her books, Gabriel Orion Marie has chosen themes that were most prominent in her journey. She created more than 325 paintings and drawings during her years in therapy and has arranged selections of them by themes for chapters. These themes and paintings are divided into three books, each sharing the subtitle *Recovery From Incest Through Painting My Story*.

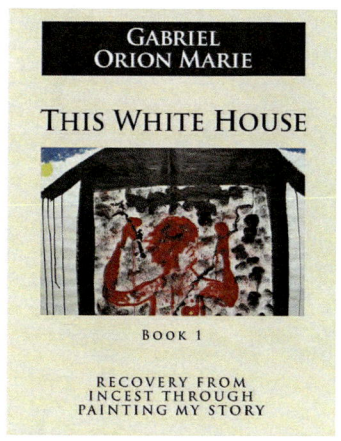

This White House (Book One) introduces you to Gabriel Orion Marie's life and the early years of her abuse, which include being sold by her father as a child prostitute and being used for child pornography. She takes you into her experience of becoming many selves (Personas) and into the abuse that drove her insane. You will come to love and admire this child/woman, and after you have been privy to what this book reveals, you will want to follow her through to recovery.

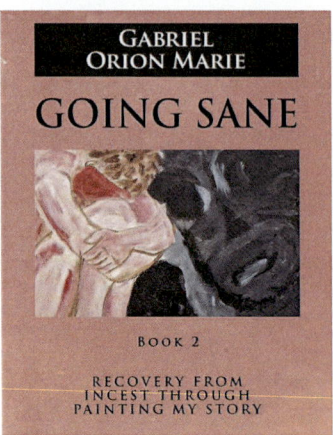

Going Sane (Book Two) takes the reader deeper into the heinous abuses and the resulting insanity that profoundly crippled and debilitated Gabriel Orion Marie. The experience of physical, emotional, and sexual tortures drove her into a depth of insanity and continual emotional trauma that permeated her daily life and required complicated and constantly shifting strategies for survival. Her tenacious courage is profoundly inspiring.

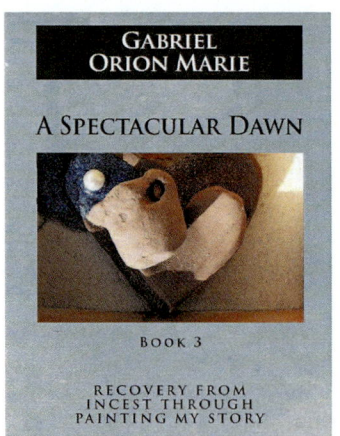

A Spectacular Dawn (Book Three) is the final in this series. Here, Gabriel Orion Marie takes you into the heart of her healing, her conscious reclaiming of her sanity, her soul, her life, and her joy. In this volume, she shares extensively from her correspondence with Dr. A., and we are allowed to witness the depth of respectful, professional love that was a key ingredient in the thoroughness of her healing.

**Visit this website for
more details and paintings:
www.GabrielOrionMarie.com**